The Caxton
Lending Library
&
Book Depository

BIBLIOMYSTERY SERIES

#1 Ken Bruen, *The Book of Virtue*, $4.95

#2 Reed Farrel Coleman, *The Book of Ghosts*, $4.95

#3 Anne Perry, *The Scroll*, $4.95

#4 Nelson DeMille, *The Book Case*, $6.95

#5 C.J. Box, *Pronghorns of the Third Reich*, $4.95

#6 William Link, *Death Leaves a Bookmark*, $4.95

#7 Jeffery Deaver, *An Acceptable Sacrifice*, $5.95

#8 Loren D. Estleman, *Book Club*, $4.95

#9 Laura Lippman, *The Book Thing*, $4.95

#10 Andrew Taylor, *The Long Sonata of the Dead*, $4.95

#11 Peter Blauner, *The Final Testament*, $4.95

#12 John Connolly, *The Caxton Lending Library & Book Depository*, $6.95

The Caxton
Lending Library
&
Book Depository

By
John Connolly

Mysterious Bookshop

New York

The Caxton Private Lending Library
& Book Depository
by John Connolly

ISBN 978-1-61316-051-0 (Limited Edition)
ISBN 978-1-61316-052-7 (Paperback)

The Caxton
Lending Library
&
Book Depository

1

*L*ET US BEGIN with this:

To those looking at his life from without, it would have seemed that Mr. Berger led a dull existence. In fact, Mr. Berger himself might well have concurred with this view.

He worked for the housing department of a minor English council, with the job title of "Closed Accounts Registrar." His task, from year to year, entailed compiling a list of those who had either relinquished or abandoned the housing provided for them by the council, and in doing so had left their accounts in arrears. Whether a week's rent was owed, or a month's, or even a year's (for evictions were a difficult business and had a habit of dragging on until relations between council and tenant came to resemble those between a besieging army and a walled city), Mr.

Berger would record the sum in question in a massive leather bound ledger known as the Closed Accounts Register. At year's end, he would then be required to balance the rents received against the rents that should have been received. If he had performed his job correctly, the difference between the two sums would be the total amount contained in the register.

Even Mr. Berger found his job tedious to explain. Rare was it for a cab driver, or a fellow passenger on a train or bus, to engage in a discussion of Mr. Berger's livelihood for longer than it took for him to describe it. Mr. Berger didn't mind. He had no illusions about himself or his work. He got on perfectly well with his colleagues, and was happy to join them for a pint of ale—but no more than that—at the end of the week. He contributed to retirement gifts, and wedding presents, and funeral wreaths. At one time it had seemed that he himself might become the cause of one such collection, for he entered into a state of cautious flirtation with a young woman in accounts. His advances appeared to be reciprocated, and the couple performed a mutual circling for the space of a year until someone less inhibited than Mr. Berger entered the fray, and the young woman, presumably weary of waiting for Mr. Berger to breach some perceived exclusion zone around her person, went off with his rival instead. It says much about Mr. Berger than he contributed to their wedding collection without a hint of bitterness.

His position as registrar paid neither badly nor particularly well, but enough to keep him clothed and fed, and maintain a roof above his head. Most of the remainder went on books. Mr. Berger led a life of the imagination, fed by stories. His flat was lined with shelves, and those shelves were filled with the books that he loved. There was no particular order to them. Oh, he kept the works of individual authors together, but he did not alphabetize, and neither did he congregate books by subject. He knew where to lay a hand on any title at any time, and that was enough. Order was for dull minds, and Mr. Berger was far less dull than he appeared (to those who are themselves unhappy, the contentment of others can sometimes be mistaken for tedium). Mr. Berger might sometimes have been a little lonely, but he was never bored, and never unhappy, and he counted his days by the books that he read.

I suppose that, in telling this tale, I have made Mr. Berger sound old. He was not. He was thirty-five and, although in no danger of being mistaken for a matinée idol, was not unattractive. Yet perhaps there was in his interiority something that rendered him, if not sexless, then somewhat oblivious to the reality of relations with the opposite sex, an impression strengthened by the collective

3

memory of what had occurred—or not oc-curred—with the girl from accounts. So it was that Mr. Berger found himself consigned to the dusty ranks of the council's spinsters and bachelors, to the army of the closeted, the odd, and the sad, al-though he was none of these things. Well, perhaps just a little of the latter: although he never spoke of it, or even fully admitted it to himself, he regret-ted his failure to express properly his affection for the girl in accounts, and had quietly resigned him-self to the possibility that a life shared with another might not be in his stars. Slowly he was becoming a kind of fixed object, and the books he read came to reflect his view of himself. He was not a great lover, and neither was he a tragic hero. Instead he resembled those narrators in fiction who observe the lives of others, existing as dowels upon which plots hang like coats until the time comes for the true actors of the book to assume them. Great and voracious reader that he was, Mr. Berger failed to realize that the life he was observing was his own.

In the autumn of 1968, on Mr. Berger's thirty-sixth birthday, the council announced that it was moving offices. Its various departments had until then been scattered like outposts throughout the city, but it now made more sense to gather them all into one purpose-built environment and sell the outlying buildings. Mr. Berger was saddened by this development. The housing department oc-

cupied a set of ramshackle offices in a redbrick ed-
ifice that had once been a private school, and there
was a pleasing oddness to the manner in which it
had been imperfectly adapted to its current role.
The council's new headquarters, meanwhile, was
a brutalist block designed by one of those acolytes
of Le Corbusier whose vision consisted solely of
purging the individual and eccentric and replacing
it with a uniformity of steel, glass and reinforced
concrete. It squatted on the site of what had once
been the city's glorious Victorian railway station,
itself now replaced by a squat bunker. In time, Mr.
Berger knew, the rest of the city's jewels would also
be turned to dust, and the ugliness of the built environment would poison the population, for how
could it be otherwise?

Mr. Berger was informed that, under the new
regimen, there would be no more need for a
Closed Accounts Register, and he would be trans-
ferred to other duties. A new, more efficient system
was to be put in place, although, as with so many
other such initiatives, it would later be revealed
that it was less efficient, and more costly, than the
original. This news coincided with the death of Mr.
Berger's elderly mother, his last surviving close rel-
ative, and the discovery of a small but significant
bequest to her son: her house, some shares, and a
sum of money that was not quite a fortune but
would, if invested carefully, enable Mr. Berger to

5

live in a degree of restrained comfort for the rest of his life. He had always had a hankering to write, and he now had the perfect opportunity to test his literary mettle.

So it was that Mr. Berger at last had a collection taken up in his name, and a small crowd gathered to bid him farewell and good luck, and he was forgotten almost as soon as he was gone.

2

Mr. Berger's mother had spent her declining years in a cottage on the outskirts of the small town of Glossom. It was one of those passingly pretty English settlements, best suited to those whose time on this earth was drawing slowly to a close, and who wanted to spend it in surroundings that were unlikely to unduly excite them, and thereby hasten the end. Its community was predominantly High Anglican, with a corresponding focus on parish-centered activities: rarely an evening went by without the church hall being occupied by amateur dramatists, or local historians, or quietly concerned Fabians.

It seemed, though, that Mr. Berger's mother had rather kept herself to herself, and few eyebrows were raised in Glossom when her son chose to do the same. He spent his days outlining his proposed work of fiction, a novel of frustrated love and muted social commentary set among the woolen mills of Lancashire in the nineteenth century. It was, Mr. Berger quickly realized, the kind of book of which the Fabians might have approved, which put something of a dampener on his progress. He dallied with some short stories instead, and when they proved similarly unrewarding he fell back on poetry, the last resort of the literary scoundrel. Finally, if only to keep his hand in, he began writing letters to the newspapers on matters of national and international concern. One, on the subject of badgers, was printed in the *Telegraph*, but it was heavily cut for publication, and Mr. Berger felt that it made him sound somewhat obsessive about badgers when nothing could be further from the truth.

It began to dawn on Mr. Berger that he might not be cut out for the life of a writer, gentleman or otherwise, and perhaps there were those who should simply be content to read. Once he had reached this conclusion, it was as though a great weight had fallen from his shoulders. He packed away the expensive writer's notebooks that he had purchased from Smythson's of Mayfair, and their weight in his pocket was replaced by the latest volume of Anthony Powell's roman fleuve, *A Dance to the Music of Time*.

In the evenings, Mr. Berger was in the habit of taking a walk by the railway line. A disused path, not far from the back gate of his cottage, led through a forest and thus to the raised bank on which the railway ran. Until recently, trains had stopped four times daily at Glossom, but the Beeching cuts had led to the closure of the station. Trains still used the lines, a noisy reminder of what had been lost, but soon even the sound of them would disappear as routes were reorganized. Eventually, the lines through Glossom would become overgrown, and the station would fall into disrepair. There were those in Glossom who had suggested buying it from British Railways and turning it into a museum, although they were unclear as to what exactly might be put in such a museum, the history of Glossom being distinctly lacking in battles, royalty, or great inventors.

None of this concerned Mr. Berger. It was enough that he had a pleasant place in which to walk or, if the weather was conducive, to sit by the lines and read. There was a stile not far from the old station, and he liked to wait there for the passing of the last train south. He would watch the businessmen in their suits flash by, and experience a surge of gratitude that his working life had reached a premature but welcome end.

Now, as winter began to close in, he still took his evening strolls, but the fading of the light and the growing chill in the air meant that he did not pause to take time with his book. Nevertheless, he always carried a volume with him, for it had become his habit to read for an hour at the Spotted Frog over a glass of wine or a pint of mild.

On the evening in question, Mr. Berger had paused as usual to wait for the train. It was, he noticed, running a little late. It had begun to do so more and more of late, which led him to wonder if all of this rationalization was really leading to any kind of improvements at all. He lit his pipe and looked to the west to witness the sun setting behind the woods, the last traces of it like flames upon the denuded branches of the trees.

It was at this point that he noticed a woman passing through the overgrown bushes a little further down the line. He had noticed before a trail of sorts there, for the branches of shrubs had been broken in places, but it was a poor substitute for his own path, and he had no desire to damage his clothing or his skin on briars. The woman was dressed in a dark dress, but what caught Berger's eye was the little red bag that she carried on her arm. It seemed in such stark contrast to the rest of her attire. He tried to see her face, but the angle of her progress concealed it from him.

At that moment he heard a distant whistle, and the stile beneath him started to vibrate. The express, the last train of the evening, was approaching. He could see its lights through the trees as it came. He looked again to his right. The woman had stopped, for she too had heard the train. Mr. Berger expected her to pause and wait for it to pass, but she did not. Instead she hastened her steps. Perhaps she wishes to be across the lines before it comes, thought Mr. Berger, but that was a risky business. It was easy to misjudge distances under such circumstances, and he had heard tales of those who had caught a foot on a sleeper, or stumbled while rushing, and the train had been the end of them.

"Ho!" he called. "Wait!"

Instinctively he stepped down from the stile and walked quickly towards her. The woman turned at the sound of his voice. Even from a distance, Mr. Berger could see that she was beautiful. Her face was pale, but she did not seem distressed. There was about her an eerie, unsettling calm.

"Don't try to cross!" he shouted. "Let the train pass."

The woman emerged from the bushes. She hitched up her skirts, showing a pair of laced ankle boots and a hint of stocking, and proceeded to climb up the embankment. Now Mr. Berger was running, but he continued to call to her, even as the express grew louder behind him before passing him in a flash of noise and light and diesel. His saw the woman cast aside her red bag, draw her head between her shoulders and, with her arms outstretched, throw herself on her knees before the train.

Mr. Berger flinched. The angle of the line meant that he did not witness the moment of impact, and any sounds of distress were lost in the roar of the engine. When he opened his eyes, the woman was gone and the train was continuing on its way.

Mr. Berger ran to the spot at which he had last seen the woman. He steeled himself for the worst, expecting to see the track mired with gore and body parts, but there was nothing. He had no experience of such matters, though, and had no idea whether a train striking a person at such a speed would leave a great mess or none at all. It was possible that the force of it had sent fragments of the woman in all directions, or even that it had carried her broken frame further down the track. After searching the bushes by the point of impact he followed the line for a time, but found no blood, and no sign of a body. He could not even find the woman's discarded red bag. Still, he had seen her, of that he had no doubt. He had not imagined it.

He was now closer to the town than he was to his home. There was no police station in Glossom, but there was one in Moreham, some five miles away. Mr. Berger walked quickly to the public telephone at the old station house, and from there he called the police and told them of what he had witnessed. Then, as instructed, he sat on the bench outside the station and waited for the patrol car to arrive.

3

The police did much the same as Mr. Berger had done, only with greater numbers and at greater expense in man-hours and overtime payments. They searched the bushes and the tracks, and enquiries were made in Glossom in case any female residents had gone missing. The driver of the train was contacted, and the train was kept on the platform at Plymouth for an hour while its engine and carriages were examined for any sign of human remains.

Finally Mr. Berger, who had remained seated on his stile throughout, was interviewed for a second time by the inspector from Moreham. His name was Carswell, and his manner when he confronted Mr. Berger was colder than it had originally been. A light rain had begun to fall shortly after the search for a body had commenced, and Carswell and his men were now damp and weary. Mr. Berger was also wet, and found that he had developed a slight but constant shiver. He suspected that he might be in shock. He had never witnessed the death of another person before. It had affected him deeply.

Now Inspector Carswell stood before him, his

hat jammed on his head and his hands thrust deep in the pockets of his coat. His men were packing up, and a pair of dogs that had been brought in to help with the search was being led back to the van in which they had arrived. The townspeople who had gathered to watch were also drifting away, but not without a final curious glance at the figure of Mr. Berger.

"Let's go through it again, shall we?" said Carswell, and Mr. Berger told his story one last time. The details remained the same. He was certain of what he had witnessed.

"I have to tell you," said Carswell, when Mr. Berger had finished speaking, "that the driver of the train saw nothing, and was unaware of any impact. As you can imagine, he was quite shocked to hear that a woman had been reported as throwing herself under his wheels. He aided in the examination of the train himself. It turns out that he has some unfortunate experience of such matters. Before he was promoted to driver, he was a fireman on an engine that struck a man near Coleford Junction. He told us that the driver saw the man on the rails but couldn't brake in time. The engine made a terrible mess of the poor fellow, he said. There was no mistaking what had happened. He seems to think that, if he had somehow hit a woman without knowing, we'd have no trouble finding her remains."

Carswell lit a cigarette. He offered one to Mr. Berger, who declined. He preferred his pipe, even though it had long since gone out.

"Do you live alone, sir?" asked Carswell.

"Yes, I do."

"From what I understand, you moved to Glossom fairly recently."

"That's correct. My mother died, and she left me her cottage."

"And you say that you're a writer?"

"Trying to be a writer. I've started to wonder if I'm really destined to be any good at it, to be honest."

"Solitary business, writing, or so I would imagine."

"It does tend to be, yes."

"You're not married?"

"No."

"Girlfriend?"

"No," said Mr. Berger, then added "Not at the moment."

He didn't want Inspector Carswell to think that there might be anything odd or unsavory about his bachelor existence.

"Ah."

Carswell drew deeply on his cigarette.

"Do you miss her?"

"Miss who?"

"Your mother."

Mr. Berger considered it an odd question to ask, but answered nonetheless.

"Of course," he said. "I would visit her when I could, and we spoke on the telephone once a week."

Carswell nodded, as if this explained a lot.

"Must be strange, coming to a new town, and living in the house in which your mother died. She passed away at home, didn't she?"

Mr. Berger thought that Inspector Carswell seemed to know a lot about his mother. Clearly he had not just been asking about a missing woman during his time in Glossom.

"Yes, she did," he replied. "Forgive me, Inspector, but what has this got to do with the death of this young woman?"

Carswell took the cigarette from his mouth and examined the burning tip, as though some answer might be found in the ash.

"I'm beginning to wonder if you might not have been mistaken in what you saw," he said.

"Mistaken? How can one be mistaken about a suicide?"

"There is no body, sir. There's no blood, no clothing, nothing. We haven't even been able to find the red bag that you mentioned. There's no sign that anything untoward happened on the track at all. So . . ."

Carswell took one last drag on his cigarette,

then dropped it on the dirt and ground it out forcefully with the heel of his shoe.

"Let's just say that you were mistaken, and leave it at that, shall we? Perhaps you might like to find some other way to occupy your evenings, now that winter is setting in. Join the bridge club, or take up singing in the choir. You might even find a young lady to walk out with. What I'm saying is, you've had a traumatic time of it, and it would be good for you not to spend so much time alone. That way, you'll avoid making mistakes of this nature again. You do understand me, don't you sir?"

The implication was clear. Being mistaken was not a crime, but wasting police time was. Mr. Berger climbed down from the stile.

"I know what I saw, Inspector," he said, but it was all that he could do to keep the doubt from creeping into his voice, and his mind was troubled as he took the path back to his little cottage.

4

It should come as no surprise to learn that Mr. Berger slept little that night. Over and over he replayed the scene of the woman's demise, and although he had neither witnessed nor heard the impact, still he saw and heard it in the silence of the bedroom. To calm himself, he had taken a large glass of his late mother's brandy upon his arrival home, but he was not used to spirits and the alcohol sat ill with him. He grew delirious in his bed, and so often did the woman's death play out before him that he began to believe that this evening was not the first time he had been present at her passing. A peculiar sense of déjà vu overcame him, one that he was entirely unable to shrug off. Sometimes, when he was ill or feverish, a tune or song would lodge itself in his mind. So entrenched would its hooks become that it would keep him from sleep, and he would be unable to exorcise it until the sickness had passed. Now he was having the same experience with his vision of the woman's death, and its repetitive nature was leading him to believe that he had already been familiar with the scene before he was present at it.

At last, thankfully, weariness overcame him and he was able to rest, but when he woke the next morning that nagging feeling of familiarity remained. He put on his coat and returned to the scene of the previous evening's excitement. He walked the rough trail, hoping to find something that the police might have missed, a sign that he had not been the victim of an overactive imagination—a scrap of black cloth, the heel of a shoe, or the red bag—but there was nothing.

It was the red bag that bothered him most of all. The red bag was the thing. With his mind unfogged by alcohol—although, in truth, his head still swam slightly in the aftermath—he grew more and more certain that the suicide of the young woman reminded him of a scene in a book: no, not just *a* scene, but perhaps *the* most famous scene of locomotive-based self-immolation in literature. He gave up on his physical search, and decided to embark on a more literary one.

He had long ago unpacked his books, although he had not yet found shelves for them all, his mother's love of reading not matching his own, and thus leading to her preference for large swathes of bare wall that she had seen fit to adorn only with cheap reproductions of sea views. There was still more room for his volumes than there had been in his own lodgings, due in no small part to the fact that the cottage had more floor space than his flat, and all a true bibliophile needs for his storage purposes is a horizontal plane. He found his copy of *Anna Karenina* sandwiched in a pile on the dining room floor between *War & Peace* and *Master and Man and Other Parables and Tales*, the latter in a nice Everyman's Library edition from 1946 about which he had forgotten, and which almost led him to set aside *Anna Karenina* in favor of a hour or so in its company. Good sense quickly prevailed, although not before he had set *Master and Man* on the dining table for further examination at a more convenient time. There it joined a dozen similarly blessed volumes, all of which had been waiting for days or weeks for their hour to come at last.

He sat in an armchair and opened *Anna Karenina* (Limited Editions Club, Cambridge, 1951, signed by Barnett Freedman, unearthed at a jumble sale in Gloucester and acquired for such a low price that Mr. Berger had later made a donation to charity in order to salve his conscience). He flipped through the pages until he found Chapter XXXI, which began with the words "A bell sounded . . ." From there he read on quickly but carefully, travelling with Anna past Piotr in his livery and top-boots, past the saucy conductor and the woman deformed, past the dirty hunchback *muzhik* until finally he came to this passage:

She was going to throw herself under the first car as its center came opposite where she stood. Her little red travelling-bag caused her to lose the moment; she could not detach it from her arm. She awaited the second. A feeling like that she had experienced once, just before taking a dive in the river, came over her, and she made the sign of the cross. This familiar gesture called back to her soul a whole series of memories of her youth and childhood; and suddenly the darkness which hid every-thing from her was torn asunder. Life, with its elusive joys, glowed for an instant before her. But she did not take her eyes from the car; and when the center, between the two wheels, appeared,

she threw away her red bag, drawing her head be-
tween her shoulders, and, with outstretched hands,
threw herself on her knees under the car. For a second
she was horror-struck at what she was doing.

"Where am I? What am I doing? Why?"

She tried to get up, to draw back; but something
monstrous, inflexible, struck her head, and threw her
on her back.

"Lord, forgive me all!" she murmured, feeling the
struggle to be in vain.

A little muzhik *was working on the railroad,*
mumbling in his beard.

And the candle by which she had read the book
that was filled with fears, with deceptions, with an-
guish, and with evil, flared up with greater brightness
than she had ever known, revealing to her all that
before was in darkness, then flickered, grew faint, and
went out forever.

Mr. Berger read the passage twice, then leaned
back in his chair and closed his eyes. It was all
there, right down to the detail of the little red bag,
the bag that the woman on the tracks had cast
aside before the express had hit her, just as Anna
had thrown away her bag before she was struck.
The woman's gestures in her final moments had
also been similar to Anna's: she too had drawn her
head between her shoulders and stretched out her
arms, as though the death to come was to take the

form of crucifixion rather than iron and wheels. Why, even Mr. Berger's own memory of the incident had been couched in similar phrases.

"My God," said Mr. Berger to the listening books, "perhaps the inspector was right and I have been spending too much time alone with only novels for company. There can be no other excuse for a man believing that he has seen the climactic scene of *Anna Karenina* reenacted on the Exeter to Plymouth railway."

He placed the volume on the arm of the chair and went to the kitchen. He was briefly tempted to reach for the brandy again, but no particular good had come of their previous shared moments, and so he opted for the routine of making a big pot of tea. When all was in place, he took a seat at the kitchen table and drank cup after cup until he had drained the pot dry. For once he did not read, nor did he distract himself with the *Times* crossword, still left untried at this late stage of the morning. He simply stared at the clouds, and listened to birdsong, and wondered if he was not, after all, going gently insane.

Mr. Berger did not read anything else that day. His two examinations of Chapter XXXI of *Anna Karenina* remained his sole contact with the world of literature. He could not recall a day when he had read less. He lived for books. They had consumed every spare moment since the revelation in childhood that he could tackle a novel alone without his mother having to read it to him. He recalled his first halting encounters with the Biggles stories of W.E. Johns, remembering how he had struggled through the longer words by breaking them up into their individual syllables, so that one difficult word became two easier ones. Ever since then, books had been his constant companions. He had, perhaps, sacrificed real friendships to these simulacra, because there were days when he had avoided his chums after school or ignored their knocking on his front door when his parents' house was otherwise empty, taking an alternative route home or staying away from the windows so that he could be sure that no football game or exploration of orchards would get in the way of finishing the story that had gripped him.

In a way, books had also been partly responsible for his fatal tentativeness with the girl from accounts. She seemed to read a little—he had seen her with a Georgette Heyer novel, and the occasional "book in brown" from the two-penny library—but he had the sense that it was not a passion with her. What if she insisted that they spend hours at the theater, or the ballet, or shopping, simply because it meant that they would be "doing things together"? That was, after all, what couples did, wasn't it? But reading was a solitary pursuit. Oh, one could read in the same room as someone else, or beside them in bed at night, but that rather presumed that an agreement had been reached about such matters, and the couple in question consisted of a pair of like-minded souls. It would be a disaster to find oneself embroiled with the sort of person who read two pages of a novel and then began humming, or tapping her fingers to attract attention, or, God help us, started fiddling with the dial on the radio. The next thing one knew, she'd be making "observations" on the text in hand, and once that happened there would be no peace for ever after.

But as he sat alone in the kitchen of his deceased mother's house, it struck Mr. Berger that he had never troubled himself to find out the views of the girl in accounts on the subject of books or, indeed, ballet. Deep inside, he had been reluctant to disturb his ordered lifestyle, a world in which he rarely had to make a more difficult decision than selecting the next book to read. He had lived his life as one removed from the world around him, and now he was paying the price in madness.

5

In the days that followed, Mr. Berger subsisted largely on newspapers and magazines of an improving nature. He had almost convinced himself that what he had seen on the tracks employed by the locomotives of the London and South Western Railway was a psychological anomaly, some form of delayed reaction to the grief he had experienced at his mother's death. He noticed that he was the object of peculiar looks, both poorly concealed and unashamedly open, as he went about his business in the town, but that was to be expected. He did hope that the town's memory of the unproductive police search might fade eventually. He had no desire to be elevated to the role of local eccentric.

But as time wore on, something odd happened. It is usually in the manner of experiences such as Mr. Berger's that, as distance grows from the event in question, so too the memory of it becomes foggier. Mr. Berger should, if the ordinary rules of behavior were being obeyed, have become ever more certain of the psychologically troubling nature of his encounter with the young woman reminiscent of Anna Karenina. But Mr. Berger found himself believing with greater and greater conviction that the opposite was true. He had seen the woman, and she was real, admittedly allowing for a certain latitude in one's definition of reality.

He began reading again, tentatively at first, but soon with his previous immersion. He also returned to walking the path that wound down to the railway line, and sitting on his stile to watch the trains go by. Each evening, with the approach of the train from Exeter to Plymouth, he would set aside his book, and watch the rougher trail to the south. It was darker now, and the trail was harder to see, but Mr. Berger's eyes were still keen, and through habit he grew practiced at picking out the difference in the density of the bushes.

But the trail remained undisturbed until February came, and the woman returned.

6

It was a cold but bracing evening. There was no damp in the air, and Mr. Berger enjoyed the sight of his breath pluming as he took his evening constitutional. There was music in the Spotted Frog that evening: some form of folk revivalism, for which Mr. Berger had a sneaking fondness. He intended to drop in for an hour or two, once he had watched the train go by. His vigil at the stile had become something of a ritual for him, and although he told himself that it was no longer connected to the business of the woman with the red bag, he secretly knew that it was. He was haunted by the image of her.

He took his seat on the stile, and lit his pipe. From somewhere to the east, he heard the sound of the approaching train. He glanced at his watch, and saw that it was just after six. The train was early. This was unheard of. If he had still been in

25

the habit of writing letters to the *Telegraph*, he might well have popped off a missive announcing this turn-up for the books, much in the manner of those twitchers who liked to let the populace know of the appearance of the first cuckoo of spring.

He was already composing the letter in his head when he was distracted by a commotion to his right. Someone was coming down the trail, and in some hurry. Mr. Berger dropped from the stile and began walking in the direction of the sounds. The sky was clear, and the moon was already silvering the undergrowth, but even without the aid of its light Mr. Berger would have been able to pick out the woman rushing to meet the train, and the red bag that hung from her arm.

Mr. Berger dropped his pipe, but managed to retrieve it. It was, after all, a good pipe.

While it would not be untrue to say that he had become obsessed with the woman, he had no real expectation of ever seeing her again. After all, people did not make a habit of throwing themselves under trains. It was the kind of act that tended to be performed once, or not at all. In the case of the former, any possible repeat of the incident was likely to be ruled out by the action of a heavy engine or, in the unlikely event of survival, sufficient recall of the painfulness of the first attempt to render most unwelcome any further repetition of it. Yet here, without a shadow of a doubt, was the same young woman carrying the same red bag and making the same rush towards self-destruction that Mr. Berger had previously witnessed.

It must be a ghost, thought Mr. Berger. There can be no other explanation. This is the spirit of some poor woman who died some time ago—for he saw that her clothing was not of this century—and she is doomed to repeat her final moments over and over until—

Until what? Mr. Berger wasn't certain. He had read his share of M.R. James and W.W. Jacobs, of Oliver Onions and William Hope Hodgson, but had never come across anything quite like this in their stories. He had a vague notion that digging up a forgotten corpse and reburying it in a more appropriate location sometimes helped, while James tended to favor restoring ancient artifacts to their previous resting place, thereby calming the spirits associated with them, but Mr. Berger had no idea where the young woman might be interred, and he had not picked so much as a flower while on his walks, let alone some old whistle or manuscript. All of this would have to be dealt with later, he realized. There was more important business to attend to.

The early arrival of the train had obviously caught the woman, spectral or otherwise, by surprise, and the branches seemed to be conspiring to keep her from her date with mortality. They caught at her dress, and at one point she took a tumble that sent her to her knees. Despite all of these hindrances, it was obvious to Mr. Berger that she was still likely to make it to the tracks in time to receive the full impact of the train.

Mr. Berger ran, and as he did so he screamed and shouted, and waved his arms. He ran faster than he had ever run before, so that he managed to reach the base of the trail some time before the woman did. She drew up short, seemingly surprised to see him. Perhaps she had been so intent on her own demise that she had failed to hear his cries, but she was now faced with the physical reality of Mr. Berger, and he with hers. She was younger than he, and her skin was unusually pale, although that might just have been the moonlight. Her hair was the blackest that Mr. Berger had ever seen. It seemed to consume the light.

The woman tried to dart to her right, and then to her left, to avoid Mr. Berger, but the bushes were too thick. He felt the ground vibrating, and the noise of the approaching train was deafeningly loud. He was aware of its whistle sounding. The driver had probably spotted him by the tracks. Mr. Berger raised his right hand and waved to let the driver know that all was okay. The woman was not going to get past him, and Mr. Berger had no intention of throwing himself under any trains.

The woman clenched her fists in frustration as

the train rushed by. Mr. Berger turned his head to watch it go, some of the passengers staring at him curiously from the window, and when he looked back the woman was gone. It was only as the rattle of the train faded that he heard the sound of bushes rustling and knew that she was making her way back up the hill. He tried to follow, but the same branches that had previously hampered her progress now delayed his. His jacket was torn, he lost his pipe, and he even twisted his left ankle slightly on a root, but he did not give up. He reached the road just in time to see the woman slip into a laneway that ran parallel to Glossom's high street. The back gardens of a row of cottages lay on one side, and on the other the rear wall of what had once been the town's brewery but was now derelict and unused, although a faint smell of old hops still hung about it.

Eventually the laneway diverged, with the path to the left eventually connecting with the main street while the path to the right twisted into darkness. Mr. Berger could see no sign of the woman to his left, for the high street was well lit. He chose instead to go right, and was soon among the relics of Glossom's industrial past: old warehouses, some still in use but most abandoned; a wall that announced the presence of a combined cooperage and chandlery, while the decay of the building behind it left no doubt that it had been some time since either barrels or candles had emerged from within; and, finally, a two-storey redbrick building with barred windows and grass growing by its doorstep. Beyond it was a dead end. As he drew nearer, Mr. Berger could have sworn that he heard a door softly closing.

Mr. Berger stood before the building and stared up at it. There were no lights burning, and the windows were so encrusted with dirt and filth both inside and out that there was no possibility of catching a glimpse of its interior. A name was carved into the brickwork above the door. Mr. Berger had to strain his eyes to read it, for the moonlight seemed to have no desire to aid him here. At last he made out the words "Caxton Private Lending Library & Book Depository."

Mr. Berger frowned. He had made enquiries in the town as to whether there was a library and had been told that there was none, the nearest, as with so much else that Glossom lacked, being in Moreham. There was a newsagent that sold books, but they were mainly detective stories and romances, and there was a limit to how many of either Mr. Berger wished to read. It was, of course, entirely likely that the Caxton Private Lending Library & Book Depository was no longer in business, but if that was the case then why was the grass growing around its doorstep trampled flat in places? Someone was still entering and leaving it on a semi-regular basis, including, if Mr. Berger was not mistaken, a woman, or something phantasmagorical that resembled a woman, with an Anna Karenina fixation.

He took out his matchbook and lit a match. There was a yellowed sign behind a small pane of glass to the right of the door. It read: "For all enquiries, please ring bell." Mr. Berger used up three matches looking in vain for a bell of any kind. There was none. Neither was there a slot or box for mail.

Mr. Berger worked his way round the corner of the building to the right, for any progress to the left was barred by the wall. Here was a smaller laneway, but it ended in another brick wall, and there were no windows on that side of the building, nor was there a door. Behind the wall was a patch of waste ground.

Mr. Berger returned to the front door. He banged on it once with his fist, more in hope than expectation of an answer. He was unsurprised when none came. He examined the single keyhole. It did not look rusted, and when he put a finger to it, the digit came back moistened with a hint of lock oil. It was all most peculiar, and not a little sinister.

There was nothing else to be done for now, Mr. Berger thought. The night was growing steadily colder, and he had not yet eaten. Although Glossom was a quiet, safe town, he did not fancy spending a long night outside a darkened lending library in the hope that a spectral woman might emerge so he could ask her what she thought she was doing, throwing herself repeatedly under trains. There were also some nasty scratches on his hands that could do with a spot of antiseptic.

So, with one final look back at the Caxton Library, and more perturbed than ever, Mr. Berger returned home, and the Spotted Frog was deprived of his custom for that night.

7

Mr. Berger returned to the Caxton Library shortly after 10.00 A.M. the next morning, on the basis that this was a reasonably civilized hour at which to appear, and if the Caxton was still in business then it was likely that someone might be about at this time. The Caxton, though, remained as silent and forbidding as it had the previous evening.

With nothing better to do, Mr. Berger began making enquiries, but to no avail. General expressions of ignorance about the nature of the Caxton Private Lending Library & Book Depository were his sole reward at the newsagent, the local grocery, and even among the early arrivals at the Spotted Frog. Oh, people seemed to be aware that the Caxton existed, but nobody was able to recall a time when it was actually in business as a lending library, nor could anyone say who owned the building, or if any books still remained inside. It was suggested that he might try the town hall in Moreham, where the records for the smaller hamlets in the vicinity were kept.

So Mr. Berger got in his car and drove to Moreham. As he drove, he considered that there seemed to be a remarkable lack of interest in the Caxton Library among the townsfolk of Glossom. It was not merely that those to whom he spoke had forgotten about its existence until Mr. Berger brought it up, at which point some faint atavistic memory of the building was uncovered before promptly being buried again; that, at least, might be understandable if the library had not been in business for many years. What was more curious was that most people seemed to be entirely unaware of its existence, and didn't care very much to investigate further once it was brought to their attention. Glossom was a close-knit community, as Mr. Berger was only too well aware, for comments about hallucinations and train delays still followed him as he asked about the library. There appeared to be only two types of business in the town: everybody's business, and business that was not yet everybody's but soon would be once the local gossips had got to work on it. The older residents of the town could provide chapter and verse on its history back to the 16th century, and every building, old or recent, had its history.

All, that is, except the Caxton Private Lending Library.

The town hall in Moreham proved to be a source of little illumination on the matter. The library building was owned by the Caxton Trust, with an address at a P.O. Box in London. The Trust paid all bills relating to the property, including rates and electricity, and that was as much as Mr. Berger could find out about it. An enquiry at the library in Moreham was met with blank looks, and although he spent hours searching back issues of the local weekly paper, the *Moreham & Glossom Advertiser*, from the turn of the century onwards, he could find no reference to the Caxton Library anywhere.

It was already dark when he returned to his cottage. He cooked himself an omelette and tried to read, but he was distracted by the fact of the library's apparent simultaneous existence and non-existence. It was there. It occupied a space in Glossom. It was a considerable building. Why, then, had its presence in a small community passed relatively unnoticed and unremarked for so long?

The next day brought no more satisfaction. Calls to booksellers and libraries, including to the grand old London Library, and the Cranston Library in Reigate, the oldest lending library in the country, confirmed only a general ignorance of the

Caxton. Finally, Mr. Berger found himself talking to the British representative of the Special Libraries Association, an organization of whose existence he had previously been unaware. She promised to search their records, but admitted that she had never heard of the Caxton and would be surprised if anyone else had either, given that her own knowledge of such matters was encyclopedic, a judgment that, after an hour-long history of libraries in England, Mr. Berger was unwilling to doubt.

Mr. Berger did consider that he might be mistaken about the woman's ultimate destination. There were other buildings in that part of town in which she could have hidden herself to escape his notice, but the Caxton was still the most likely place in which she might have sought refuge. Where else, he thought, would a woman intent upon repeatedly reenacting the final moments of Anna Karenina choose to hide but an old library?

He made his decision before he went to bed that night. He would become a detective of sorts, and stake out the Caxton Private Lending Library & Book Depository for as long as it took for it to reveal its secrets to him.

8

As Mr. Berger soon discovered, it was no easy business being a detective on a stakeout. It was all very well for those chaps in books who could sit in a car or a restaurant and make observations about the world in a degree of comfort, especially if they were in Los Angeles or somewhere else with a climate noted for warmth and sunlight. It was quite another thing to hang around among dilapidated buildings in a small English town on a cold, damp February day, hoping that nobody one knew happened by or, worse, some passing busybody didn't take it upon himself to phone the police and report a loiterer. Mr. Berger could just imagine Inspector Carswell smoking another cigarette and concluding that he now most definitely had some form of lunatic on his hands.

Thankfully, Mr. Berger found a sheltered space in the old cooperage and chandlery that afforded a view of the end of the laneway through a collapsed section of wall while allowing him to remain relatively concealed. He had brought a blanket, a cushion, a flask of tea, some sandwiches and chocolate, and two books, one of them a John Dickson Carr novel entitled *The Crooked Hinge*, just to enter into the spirit of the thing, and the other *Our Mutual Friend* by Charles Dickens, the only Dickens he had yet to read. *The Crooked Hinge* turned out to be rather good, if a little fantastical. Then again, Mr. Berger considered, a tale of witchcraft and automatons was hardly more outlandish than apparently witnessing the same

36

woman attempt suicide twice, the first time suc-
cessfully and the second time less so.

The day passed without incident. There was no
activity in the laneway, the rustle of the odd rat
apart. Mr. Berger finished the Dickson Carr and
started the Dickens, which, being the author's last
completed novel, meant that it was mature Dickens, and hence rather difficult by the standards of
Oliver Twist or *The Pickwick Papers*, and requiring
considerably more patience and attention. When
the light began to fade, Mr. Berger set aside the
book, unwilling to risk drawing attention by using
a torch, and waited another hour in the hope that
darkness might bring with it some activity at the
Caxton Library. No illumination showed in the old
building, and Mr. Berger eventually gave up the
watch for the night, and took himself to the Spotted Frog for a hot meal and a restorative glass of
wine.

His vigil recommenced early the next morning,
although he chose to alternate Dickens with Wode-
house. Once again, the day passed with little excitement, the appearance of a small terrier dog
apart. The dog began yapping at Mr. Berger, who
shooed it ineffectually until its owner gave a shrill
whistle from nearby and the dog departed. Still,
the day was warmer than the one before, which
was a small blessing: Mr. Berger had woken that
morning with stiff limbs, and had determined to

wear two overcoats if the new day proved as chilly as the last.

Darkness started to descend, and with it doubts on the part of Mr. Berger about the wisdom of his course of action. He couldn't hang around laneways indefinitely. It was unseemly. He leaned into a corner and found himself starting to doze. He dreamed of lights in the Caxton Library, and a train that rolled down the laneway, its complement of passengers consisting entirely of dark-haired ladies carrying small red bags, all of them steeling themselves for self-destruction. Finally he dreamed of footsteps on gravel and grass, but when he woke he could still hear the footsteps. Someone was coming. Tentatively he rose from his resting place and peered at the library. There was a figure on its doorstep carrying what looked like a carpet bag, and he heard the rattle of keys.

Instantly Mr. Berger was on his feet. He climbed through the gap in the wall and emerged into the laneway. An elderly man was standing before the door of the Caxton Library, his key already turning in the lock. He was shorter than average, and wore a long grey overcoat and a trilby hat with a white feather in the band. A remarkable silver handlebar mustache adorned his upper lip. He looked at Mr. Berger with some alarm and hurriedly opened the door.

"Wait!" said Mr. Berger. "I have to talk to you."

The old gent was clearly in no mood to talk. The door was wide open now, and he was already inside when he realized that he had forgotten his carpet bag, which remained on the ground. He reached for it, but Mr. Berger got there at the same time, and an unseemly tug-of-war began with each man holding on to one of the straps.

"Hand it over!" said the old man.

"No," said Mr. Berger. "I want to talk with you."

"You'll have to make an appointment. You'll need to telephone in advance."

"There's no number. You're not listed."

"Then send a letter."

"You don't have a postbox."

"Look, you must come back tomorrow and ring the bell."

"There is no bell!" shouted Mr. Berger, his frustration getting the better of him as his voice jumped an octave. He gave a final hard yank on the bag and won the struggle, leaving only a handle in the grip of the old man.

"Oh, bother!" said the old man. He looked wistfully at his bag, which Mr. Berger was clutching to his chest. "I suppose you'd better come in, then, but you can't stay long. I'm a very busy man."

He stepped back, inviting Mr. Berger to enter. Now that the opportunity had at last presented itself, that worthy gentleman experienced a twinge of concern. The interior of the Caxton Library looked very dark, and who knew what might be waiting inside? He was throwing himself at the mercy of a possible madman, armed only with a hostage carpet bag. But he had come this far in his investigation, and he required an answer of some sort if he was ever to have peace of mind again. Still holding on to the carpet bag as though it were a swaddled infant, he stepped into the library.

9

Lights came on. They were dim, and the illumination they offered had a touch of jaundice to it, but they revealed lines of shelves stretching off into the distance, and that peculiar musty smell distinctive to rooms in which books are aging like fine wines. To his left was an oak counter, and behind it cubbyholes filled with paperwork that appeared not to have been touched in many years, for a fine film of dust lay over it all. Beyond the counter was an open door, and through it Mr. Berger could see a small living area with a television, and the edge of a bed in an adjoining room.

The old gent removed his hat, and his coat and scarf, and hung them on a hook by the door. Beneath them he was wearing a dark suit of considerable vintage, a white shirt, and a very wide gray-and-white striped tie. He looked rather dapper, in a slightly decaying way. He waited patiently for Mr. Berger to begin, which Mr. Berger duly did.

"Look," said Mr. Berger, "I won't have it. I simply won't."

"Won't have what?"

"Women throwing themselves under trains, then coming back and trying to do it again. It's just not on. Am I making myself clear?"

The elderly gentleman frowned. He tugged at one end of his mustache and sighed deeply.

"May I have my bag back, please?" he asked.

Mr. Berger handed it over, and the old man stepped behind the counter and placed the bag in the living room before returning. By this time, though, Mr. Berger, in the manner of bibliophiles everywhere, had begun to examine the contents of the nearest shelf. The shelves were organized alphabetically, and by chance Mr. Berger had started on the letter 'D'. He discovered an incomplete collection of Dickens' work, seemingly limited to the best known of the writer's works. *Our Mutual Friend* was conspicuously absent, but *Oliver Twist* was present, as were *David Copperfield*, *A Tale of Two Cities*, *Pickwick Papers*, and a handful of others. All of the editions looked very old. He took *Oliver Twist* from the shelf and examined its points. It was bound in brown cloth with gilt lettering and bore the publisher's imprint at the foot of the spine. The title page attributed the work to

Boz, not Charles Dickens, indicating a very early edition, a fact confirmed by the date of publisher and date of publication: Richard Bentley, London, 1838. Mr. Berger was holding the first edition, first issue, of the novel.

"Please be careful with that," said the old gent, who was hovering nervously nearby, but Mr. Berger had already replaced *Oliver Twist* and was now examining *A Tale of Two Cities*, perhaps his favorite novel by Dickens: Chapman & Hall, 1859, original red cloth. It was another first edition.

But it was the volume marked *Pickwick Papers* that contained the greatest surprise. It was over-sized, and contained within it not a published copy but a manuscript. Mr. Berger knew that most of Dickens' manuscripts were held by the Victoria & Albert Museum as part of the Forster Collection, for he had seen them when they were last on display. The rest were held by the British Library, the Wisbech Museum, and the Morgan Library in New York. Fragments of *Pickwick Papers* formed part of the collection of the New York Public Library, but as far as Mr. Berger was aware, there was no complete manuscript of the book anywhere.

Except, it seemed, in the Caxton Private Lending Library & Book Depository of Glossom, England.

"Is it—?" said Mr. Berger. "I mean, can it—?"

The old gentleman gently removed the volume from Mr. Berger's hands and placed it back in its place on the shelf.

"Indeed," said the gentleman.

He was looking at Mr. Berger a little more thoughtfully than before, as though his visitor's obvious appreciation for the books had prompted a reassessment of his probable character.

"It's in rather good company as well," he said.

He gestured expansively at the rows of shelves. They stretched into the gloom, for the yellow lights had not come on in the farther reaches of the library. There were also doors leading off to the left and right. They were set into the main walls, but Mr. Berger had seen no doors when he had first examined the building. They could have been bricked up, but he had seen no evidence of that either.

"Are they all first editions?" he asked.

"First editions, or manuscript copies. First editions are fine for our purposes, though. Manuscripts are merely a bonus."

"I should like to look, if you don't mind," said Mr. Berger. "I won't touch any more of them. I'd just like to see them."

"Later, perhaps," said the gent. "You still haven't told me why you're here."

Mr. Berger swallowed hard. He had not spoken aloud of his encounters since the unfortunate con-

43

versation with Inspector Carswell on that first night.

"Well," he said, "I saw a woman commit suicide in front of a train, and then some time later I saw her try to do the same thing again, but I stopped her. I thought she might have come in here. In fact, I'm almost certain that she did."

"That is unusual," said the gent.

"That's what I thought," said Mr. Berger.

"And do you have any idea of this woman's identity?"

"Not exactly," said Mr. Berger.

"Would you care to speculate?"

"It will seem odd."

"No doubt."

"You may think me mad."

"My dear fellow, we hardly know each other. I wouldn't dare to make such a judgment until we were better acquainted."

Which seemed fair enough to Mr. Berger. He had come this far: he might as well finish the journey.

"It did strike me that she might be Anna Karenina." At the last minute, Mr. Berger hedged his bets. "Or a ghost, although she did appear remarkably solid for a spirit."

"She wasn't a ghost," said the gent.

"No, I didn't really believe so. There was the issue of her substantiality. I suppose you'll tell me

44

now that she wasn't Anna Karenina either."

The old gent tugged at his mustache again. His face was betrayed his thoughts as he carried on an internal debate with himself.

Finally, he said "No, in all conscience I could not deny that she is Anna Karenina."

Mr. Berger leaned in closer, and lowered his voice significantly. "Is she a loony? You know . . . someone who thinks that she's Anna Karenina?"

"No. You're the one who thinks that she's Anna Karenina, but she *knows* that she's Anna Karenina."

"What?" said Mr. Berger, somewhat thrown by the reply. "So you mean she *is* Anna Karenina? But Anna Karenina is simply a character in a book by Tolstoy. She isn't real."

"But you just told me that she was."

"No, I told you that the woman I saw *seemed* real."

"And that you thought she might be Anna Karenina."

"Yes, but you see, it's all very well saying that to oneself, or even presenting it as a possibility, but one does so in the hope that a more rational explanation might present itself."

"But there isn't a more rational explanation, is there?"

"There might be," said Mr. Berger. "I just can't think of one at present."

Mr. Berger was starting to feel light-headed.

"Would you like a cup of tea?" said the old gent.

"Yes," said Mr. Berger, "I rather think I would."

10

They sat in the gentleman's living room, drinking tea from china cups and eating some fruitcake that he kept in a tin. A fire had been lit, and a lamp burned in a corner. The walls were decorated with oils and watercolors, all of them very fine and very old. The style of a number of them was familiar to Mr. Berger. He wouldn't have liked to swear upon it, but he was fairly sure that there was at least one Turner, a Constable, and two Romneys, a portrait and a landscape, among their number.

The old gentleman had introduced himself as Mr. Gedeon, and he had been the librarian at the Caxton for more than forty years. His job, he informed Mr. Berger, was "to maintain and, as required, increase the collection; to perform restorative work on the volumes where necessary; and, of course, to look after the characters."

It was this last phrase that made Mr. Berger choke slightly on his tea.

"The characters?" he said.

"The characters," confirmed Mr. Gedeon.

"What characters?"

"The characters from the novels."

"You mean: they're alive?"

Mr. Berger was beginning to wonder not only about his own sanity but that of Mr. Gedeon as well. He felt as though he had wandered into some strange bibliophilic nightmare. He kept hoping that he would wake up at home with a headache to find that he had been inhaling gum from one of his own volumes.

"You saw one of them," said Mr. Gedeon.

"Well, I saw someone," said Mr. Berger. "I mean, I've seen chaps dressed up as Napoleon at parties, but I didn't go home thinking I'd met Napoleon."

"We don't have Napoleon," said Mr. Gedeon.

"No?"

"No. Only fictional characters here. It gets a little complicated with Shakespeare, I must admit. That's caused us some problems. The rules aren't hard and fast. If they were, this whole business would run a lot more smoothly. But then, literature isn't a matter of rules, is it? Think how dull it would be if it was, eh?"

Mr. Berger peered into his teacup, as though expecting the arrangement of the leaves to reveal the truth of things. When they did not, he put the cup down, clasped his hands, and resigned himself to whatever was to come.

"All right," he said. "Tell me about the characters . . ."

It was, said Mr. Gedeon, all to do with the public. At some point, certain characters became so familiar to readers—and, indeed, to many non-readers—that they reached a state of existence independent of the page.

"Take Oliver Twist, for example," said Mr. Gedeon. "More people know of Oliver Twist than have ever read the work to which he gave his name. The same is true for Romeo and Juliet, and Robinson Crusoe, and Don Quixote. Mention their names to the even averagely educated man or woman on the street and, regardless of whether they've ever encountered a word of the texts in question, they'll be able to tell you that Romeo and Juliet were doomed lovers, that Robinson Crusoe was marooned on an island, and Don Quixote was involved in some business with windmills. Similarly, they'll tell you that Macbeth got above himself, that Ebenezer Scrooge came right in the end, and that D'Artagnan, Athos, Aramis and Porthos were the names of the musketeers.

"Admittedly, there's a limit to the number of those who achieve that kind of familiarity. They end up here as a matter of course. But you'd be surprised by how many people can tell you something of Tristram Shandy, or Tom Jones, or Jay Gatsby. I'm not sure where the point of crossover is, to be perfectly honest. All I know is that, at some point, a character becomes sufficiently famous to pop into existence and, when they do so, they materialize in or near the Caxton Private Lending Library & Book Depository. They always have, ever since the original Mr. Caxton set up the first depository shortly before his death in 1492. According to the history of the library, he did so when some of Chaucer's pilgrims turned up on his doorstep in 1477."

"Some of them?" said Mr. Berger. "Not all?"

"Nobody remembers all of them," said Mr. Gedeon. "Caxton found the Miller, the Reeve, the Knight, the Second Nun, and the Wife of Bath all arguing in his yard. Once he became convinced that they were not actors or lunatics, he realized that he had to find somewhere to keep them. He didn't want to be accused of sorcery or any other such nonsense, and he had his enemies: where there are books, there will always be haters of books alongside the lovers of them.

"So Caxton found a house in the country for them, and this also served as a library for parts of his own collection. He even established a means of continuing to fund the library after he was gone, one that continues to be used to this day. Basically, we mark up what should be marked down, and mark down what should be marked up, and the difference is deposited with the Trust."

"I'm not sure that I understand," said Mr. Berger.

"It's simple, really. It's all to do with ha'pennys, and portions of cents, or lire, or whatever the currency may be. If, say, a writer was due to be paid the sum of nine pounds, ten shillings, and sixpence ha'penny in royalties, the ha'penny would be shaved off and given to us. Similarly, if a company owes a publisher seventeen pounds, eight shillings and sevenpence ha'penny, they're charged eight-pence instead. This goes on all through the industry, even down to individual books sold. Sometimes we're dealing in only fractions of a penny, but when we take them from all round the world and add them together, it's more than enough to fund the Trust, maintain the library, and house the characters here. It's now so embedded in the system of books and publishing that nobody even notices anymore."

Mr. Berger was troubled. He would have had no time for such accounting chicanery when it came to the Closed Accounts Register. It did make sense, though.

"And what is the Trust?"

"Oh, the Trust is just a name that's used for convenience. There hasn't been an actual Trust in years, or not one on which anyone sits. For all intents and purposes, this is the Trust. I am the Trust. When I pass on, the next librarian will be the Trust. There's not much work to it. I rarely even have to sign checks."

While the financial support structure for the library was all very interesting, Mr. Berger was more interested in the question of the characters.

"To get back to these characters, they live here?"

"Oh, absolutely. As I explained, they just show up outside when the time is right. Some are obviously a little confused, but it all becomes clear to them in the days that follow, and they start settling in. And when they arrive, so too does a first edition of the relevant work, wrapped in brown paper and tied with string. We put in on a shelf and keep it nice and safe. It's their life story, and it has to be preserved. Their history is fixed in those pages."

"What happens with series characters?" asked Mr. Berger. "Sherlock Holmes, for example? Er, I'm assuming he's here somewhere."

"Of course," said Mr. Gedeon. "We numbered his rooms as 221B, just to make him feel at home. Dr. Watson lives next door. In their case, I do believe that the library received an entire collection of first editions of the canonical works."

"The Conan Doyle books, you mean?"

"Yes. Nothing after Conan Doyle's death in 1930 actually counts. It's the same for all of the iconic characters here. Once the original creator passes on, then that's the end of their story as far as we, and they, are concerned. Books by other authors who take up the characters don't count. It would all be unmanageable otherwise. Needless to say, they don't show up here until after their creators have died. Until then, they're still open to change."

"I'm finding all of this extremely difficult to take in," said Mr. Berger.

"Dear fellow," said Mr. Gedeon, leaning over and patting Mr. Berger's arm reassuringly, "don't imagine for a moment that you're the first. I felt exactly the same way the first time that I came here."

"How did you come here?"

"I met Hamlet at a number 48B bus stop," said Mr. Gedeon. "He'd been there for some time, poor chap. At least eight buses had passed him by, and he hadn't taken any of them. It's to be expected, I suppose. It's in his nature."

"So what did you do?"

"I got talking to him, although he does tend to soliloquize so one has to be patient. Saying it aloud, I suppose it seems nonsensical in retrospect that I wouldn't simply have called the police and told them that a disturbed person who was under the impression he was Hamlet was marooned at the 48B bus stop. But I've always loved Shakespeare, you see, and I found the man at the bus stop quite fascinating. By the time he'd finished speaking, I was convinced. I brought him back here and restored him to the safe care of the librarian of the day. That was old Headley, my predecessor. I had a cup of tea with him, much as we're doing now, and that was the start of it. When Headley retired, I took his place. Simple as that."

It didn't strike Mr. Berger as very simple at all. It seemed complicated on a quite cosmic scale.

"Could I—?" Mr. Berger began to say, then stopped. It struck him as a most extraordinary thing to ask, and he wasn't sure that he should.

"See them?" said Mr. Gedeon. "By all means! Best bring your coat, though. I find it can get a bit chilly back there."

Mr. Berger did as he was told. He put on his coat and followed Mr. Gedeon past the shelves, his eyes taking in the titles as he went. He wanted to touch the books, to take them down and stroke them, like cats, but he controlled the urge. After all, if Mr. Gedeon was to be believed, he was about to have a far more extraordinary encounter with the world of books.

11

In the end, it proved to be slightly duller than Mr. Berger had expected. Each of the characters had a small but clean suite of rooms, personalized to suit their time periods and dispositions. Mr. Gedeon explained that they didn't organize the living areas by authors or periods of history, so there weren't entire wings devoted to Dickens or Shakespeare.

"It just didn't work when it was tried in the past," said Mr. Gedeon. "Worse, it caused terrible problems, and some awful fights. The characters tend to have a pretty good instinct for these things themselves, and my inclination has always been to let them choose their own space."

They passed Room 221B where Sherlock Holmes appeared to be in an entirely drug-induced state of stupor, while in a nearby suite Tom Jones was doing something unspeakable with Fanny Hill. There was a brooding Heathcliff, and a Fagin with rope burns around his neck, but like animals in a zoo, a lot of the characters were simply napping.

"They do that a lot," said Mr. Gedeon. "I've seen some of them sleep for years, decades even. They don't get hungry as such, although they do like to eat to break the monotony. Force of habit, I suppose. We try to keep them away from wine. That makes them rowdy."

"But do they realize that they're fictional characters?" said Mr. Berger.

"Oh, yes. Some of them take it better than others, but they all learn to accept that their lives have been written by someone else, and their memories are a product of literary invention, even if, as I said

54

earlier, it gets a bit more complicated with historical characters."

"But you said it was only fictional characters who ended up here," Mr. Berger protested.

"That is the case, as a rule, but it's also true that some historical characters become more real to us in their fictional forms. Take Richard III: much of the public perception of him is a product of Shakespeare's play and Tudor propaganda, so in a sense that Richard III *is* a fictional character. Our Richard III is aware that he's not actually *the* Richard III but *a* Richard III. On the other hand, as far as the public is concerned he is *the* Richard III, and is more real in their minds than any products of later revisionism. But he's the exception rather than the rule: very few historical characters manage to make that transition. All for the best, really, otherwise this place would be packed to the rafters."

Mr. Berger had wanted to raise the issue of space with the librarian, and this seemed like the opportune moment.

"I did notice that the building seems significantly larger on the inside than on the outside," he remarked.

"It's funny, that," said Mr. Gedeon. "Doesn't seem to matter much what the building looks like on the outside: it's as though, when they all move in, they bring their own space with them. I've often wondered why that might be, and I think I've come up with an answer of sorts. It's a natural consequence of the capacity of a bookstore or library to contain entire worlds, whole universes, and all contained between the covers of books. In that sense, every library or bookstore is practically infinite. This library takes that to its logical conclusion."

They passed a pair of overly ornate and decidedly gloomy rooms, in one of which an ashen-faced man sat reading a book, his unusually long fingernails gently testing the pages. He turned to watch them pass, and his lips drew back to reveal a pair of elongated canines.

"The Count," said Mr. Gedeon, in a worried manner. "I'd move along if I were you."

"You mean Stoker's Count?" said Mr. Berger. He couldn't help but gawp. The Count's eyes were rimmed with red, and there was an undeniable magnetism to him. Mr. Berger found his feet dragging him into the room as the Count set aside his book and prepared to welcome him.

Mr. Gedeon's hand grasped his right arm and pulled him back into the corridor.

"I told you to move along," he said. "You don't want to be spending time with the Count. Very unpredictable, the Count. Says he's over all that vampiric nonsense, but I wouldn't trust him farther than I could throw him."

"He can't get out, can he?" asked Mr. Berger, who was already rethinking his passion for evening walks.

"No, he's one of the special cases. We keep those books behind bars, and that seems to do the trick for the characters as well."

"But some of the others wander," said Mr. Berger. "You met Hamlet, and I met Anna Karenina."

"Yes, but that's really most unusual. For the most part, the characters exist in a kind of stasis. I suspect a lot of them just close their eyes and relive their entire literary lives, over and over. Still, we do have quite a competitive bridge tournament going, and the pantomime at Christmas is always good fun."

"How do they get out, the ones who ramble off?"

Mr. Gedeon shrugged. "I don't know. I keep the place well locked up, and it's rare that I'm not here. I just took a few days off to visit my brother in Bootle, but I've probably never spent more than a month in total away from the library in all of my years as librarian. Why would I? I've got books to read, and characters to talk to. I've got worlds to explore, all within these walls."

At last they reached a closed door upon which Mr. Gedeon knocked tentatively.

"*Oui?*" said a female voice.

"*Madame, vous avez un visiteur,*" said Mr. Gedeon.

"*Bien. Entrez, s'il vous plaît.*"

Mr. Gedeon opened the door, and there was the woman whom Mr. Berger had watched throw herself beneath the wheels of a train, and whose life he felt that he had subsequently saved, sort of. She was wearing a simple black dress, perhaps even the very one that had so captivated Kitty in the novel, her curly hair in disarray, and a string of pearls hanging around her firm neck. She seemed startled at first to see him, and he knew that she recalled his face.

Mr. Berger's French was a little rusty, but he managed to dredge up a little from memory.

"*Madame, je m'appelle Monsieur Berger, et je suis enchanté de vous rencontrer.*"

"*Non,*" said Anna, after a short pause, "*tout le plaisir est pour moi, Monsieur Berger. Vous vous assiérez, s'il vous plaît.*"

He took a seat, and a polite conversation commenced. Mr. Berger explained, in the most delicate terms, that he had been a witness to her earlier encounter with the train, and it had haunted him. Anna appeared most distressed, and apologized profusely for any trouble that she might have caused him, but Mr. Berger waved it away as purely minor, and stressed that he was more concerned for her than for himself. Naturally, he said, when he saw her

58

making a second attempt—if attempt was the right word for an act that had been so successful first time round—he had felt compelled to intervene.

After some initial hesitancy, their conversation grew easier. At some point Mr. Gedeon arrived with more tea, and some more cake, but they barely noticed him. Mr. Berger found much of his French returning, but Anna, having spent so long in the environs of the library, also had a good command of English. They spoke together long into the night, until at last Mr. Berger noticed the hour, and apologized for keeping Anna up so late. She replied that she had enjoyed his company, and she slept little anyway. He kissed her hand, and begged leave to return the next day, and she gave her permission willingly.

Mr. Berger found his way back to the library without too much trouble, apart from an attempt by Fagin to steal his wallet, which the old reprobate put down to habit and nothing more. When he reached Mr. Gedeon's living quarters, he discovered the librarian dozing in an armchair. He woke him gently, and Mr. Gedeon opened the front door to let him out.

"If you wouldn't mind," said Mr. Berger, as he stood on the doorstep, "I should very much like to return tomorrow to speak with you, and Ms. Karenina, if that wouldn't be too much of an imposition."

"It wouldn't be an imposition at all," said Mr. Gedeon. "Just knock on the glass. I'll be here."

With that the door was closed, and Mr. Berger, feeling both more confused and more elated than he had in all his life, returned to his cottage in the darkness, and slept a deep, dreamless sleep.

12

The next morning, once he had washed and breakfasted, Mr. Berger returned to the Caxton Library. He brought with him some fresh pastries that he had bought in the local bakery in order to replenish Mr. Gedeon's supplies, and a book of Russian poetry in translation of which he was unusually fond, but which he now desired to present to Anna. Making sure that he was not being observed, he took the laneway that led to the library and knocked on the glass. He was briefly fearful that Mr. Gedeon might have spirited away the contents of the premises—books, characters, and all—overnight, fearful that the discovery by Mr. Berger of the library's true nature might bring some trouble upon them all, but the old gentleman opened the door to Mr. Berger's knock on the glass and seemed very pleased to see him return.

"Will you take some tea?" asked Mr. Gedeon, and Mr. Berger agreed, even though he had already had tea at breakfast and was anxious to return to

Anna. Still, he had questions for Mr. Gedeon, particularly pertaining to Anna.

"Why does she do it?" he asked, as he and Mr. Gedeon shared an apple scone between them.

"Do what?" said Mr. Gedeon. "Oh, you mean throw herself under trains?"

He picked a crumb from his waistcoat and put it on his plate.

"First of all, I should say that she doesn't make a habit of it," said Mr. Gedeon. "In all the years that I've been here, she's done it no more than a dozen times. Admittedly, the incidents have been growing more frequent, and I have spoken to her about them in an effort to find some way to help, but she doesn't seem to know herself why she feels compelled to relive her final moments in the book. We have other characters that return to their fates— just about all of our Thomas Hardy characters appear obsessed by them—but she's the only one who reenacts her end. I can only give you my thoughts on the matter, and I'd say this: she's the titular character, and her life is so tragic, her fate so awful, that it could be that both are imprinted upon the reader, and herself, in a particularly deep and resonant way. It's in the quality of the writing. It's in the book. Books have power. You must understand that now. It's why we keep all of these first editions so carefully. The fate of characters is set forever in those volumes. There's a link between those editions and the characters that arrived here with them."

He shifted in his chair, and pursed his lips.

"I'll share something with you, Mr. Berger, something that I've never shared with anyone before," he said. "Some years ago, we had a leak in the roof. It wasn't a big one, but they don't need to be big, do they? A little water dripping for hours and hours can do a great deal of damage, and it wasn't until I got back from the picture house in Moreham that I saw what had happened. You see, before I left I'd set aside our manuscript copies of *Alice in Wonderland* and *Moby Dick.*"

"*Moby Dick*?" said Mr. Berger. "I wasn't aware that there were any extant manuscripts of *Moby Dick.*"

"It's an unusual one, I'll admit," said Mr. Gedeon. "Somehow it's all tied up with confusion between the American and British first editions. The American edition, by Harper & Brothers, was set from the manuscript, and the British edition, by Bentley's, was in turn set from the American proofs, but there are some six hundred differences in wording between the two editions. But in 1851, while Melville was working on the British edition based on proofs that he himself had paid to be set and plated before an American publisher had signed an agreement, he was also still writing some of the later parts of the book, and in addition he took the opportunity to rewrite sections that had already been set for America. So which is the edition that the library should store: the American, based on the original manuscript, or the British, based not on the manuscript but on a subsequent rewrite? The decision made by the Trust was to acquire the British edition and, just to be on the safe side, the manuscript. When Captain Ahab arrived at the Library, both editions arrived with him."

"And the manuscript of *Alice in Wonderland*? I understood that to be in the collection of the British Museum."

"Some sleight-of-hand there, I believe," said Mr. Gedeon. "You may recall that the Reverend Dodgson gave the original ninety-page manuscript to Alice Liddell, but she was forced to sell it in order to pay death duties following her husband's death in 1928. Sotheby's sold it on her behalf, suggesting a reserve of four thousand pounds. It went, of course, for almost four times that amount, to an American bidder. At that point, the Trust stepped in, and a similar manuscript copy was substituted and sent to the United States."

"So the British Museum now holds a fake?"

"Not a fake, but a later copy, made by Dodgson's hand at the Trust's instigation. In those days, the Trust was always thinking ahead, and I've tried to keep up that tradition. I've always got an eye out for a book or character that may be taking off.

63

"So the Trust was very keen to have Dodgson's original *Alice*: so many iconic characters, you see, and then there were the illustrations too. It's an extremely powerful manuscript.

"But all of this is beside the point. Both of the manuscripts needed a bit of attention—just a careful clean to remove any dust or other media with a little polyester film. Well, I almost cried when I returned to the library. Some of the water from the ceiling had fallen on the manuscripts: just drops, nothing more, but enough to send some of the ink from *Moby Dick* on to a page of the *Alice* manuscript."

"And what happened?" asked Mr. Berger.

"For one day, in all extant copies of *Alice in Wonderland*, there was a whale at the Mad Hatter's tea party," said Mr. Gedeon solemnly.

"What? I don't remember that."

"Nobody does, nobody but I. I worked all day to clean the relevant section, and gradually removed all traces of Melville's ink. *Alice in Wonderland* went back to the way it was before, but for that day every copy of the book, and all critical commentaries on it, noted the presence of a white whale at the tea party."

"Good grief! So the books can be changed?"

"Only the copies contained in the library's collection, and they in turn affect all others. This is not just a library, Mr. Berger: it's the *ur*-library. It has to do with the rarity of the books in its collection and their links to the characters. That's why we're so careful with them. We have to be. No book is really a fixed object. Every reader reads a book differently, and each book works in a different way on each reader. But the books here are special. They're the books from which all later copies came. I tell you, Mr. Berger, not a day goes by in this place that doesn't bring me one surprise or another, and that's the truth."

But Mr. Berger was no longer listening. He was thinking again of Anna and the awfulness of those final moments as the train approached, of her fear and her pain, and how she seemed doomed to repeat them because of the power of the book to which she had given her name.

But the contents of the books were not fixed. They were open not just to differing interpretations, but to actual change.

Fates could be altered.

13

Mr. Berger did not act instantly. He had never considered himself a duplicitous individual, and he tried to tell himself that his actions in gaining Mr. Gedeon's confidence were as much to do with his enjoyment of that gentleman's company, and his fascination with the Caxton's contents, as with any desire he might have harbored to save Anna Karenina from further fatal encounters with loco-motives.

There was more than a grain of truth to this. Mr. Berger did enjoy spending time with Mr. Gedeon, for the librarian was a vast repository of information about the library and the history of his predecessors in the role. Similarly, no biblio-phile could fail to be entranced by the library's in-ventory, and each day among its stacks brought new treasures to light, some of which had been ac-quired purely for their rarity value rather than be-cause of any particular character link: annotated manuscripts dating back to the birth of the printed word, including poetical works by Donne, Marvell, and Spenser; not one but two copies of the First Folio of Shakespeare's works, one of them belong-ing to Edward Knight himself, the book-holder of the King's Men and the presumed proofreader of the manuscript sources for the Folio, and contain-ing his handwritten corrections to the errors that had crept into his particular edition, for the Folio was still being proofread during the printing of the book, and there were variances between individual copies; and what Mr. Berger suspected might well be notes, in Dickens's own hand, for the later, un-completed chapters of *The Mystery of Edwin Drood.*

This latter artifact was discovered by Mr. Berger

in an uncatalogued file that also contained an abandoned version of the final chapters of F. Scott Fitzgerald's *The Great Gatsby,* in which Gatsby, not Daisy, is behind the wheel when Myrtle is killed. Mr. Berger had glimpsed Gatsby briefly on his way to visit Anna Karenina. By one of the miracles of the library, Gatsby's quarters appeared to consist of a pool house and a swimming pool, although the pool was made marginally less welcoming by the presence in it of a deflated, bloodstained mattress.

The sight of Gatsby, who was pleasant but haunted, and the discovery of an alternate ending to the book to which Gatsby, like Anna, had given his name, caused Mr. Berger to wonder what might have happened had Fitzgerald published the version held by the Caxton instead of the book that eventually appeared, in which Daisy is driving the car on that fateful night. Would it have altered Gatsby's eventual fate? Probably not, he decided: there would still have been a bloodstained mattress in the swimming pool, but Gatsby's end would have been rendered less tragic, and less noble.

But the fact that he could even think in this way about endings that might have been confirmed in him the belief that Anna's fate might be altered, and so it was that he began to spend more and more time in the section devoted to Tolstoy's works, and familiarized himself with the history of *Anna*

Karenina. His researches revealed that even this novel, described as "flawless" by both Dostoevsky and Nabokov, presented problems when it came to its earliest appearance. While it was originally published in installments in the *Russian Messenger* periodical from 1873 onwards, an editorial dispute over the final part of the story meant that it did not appear in its complete form until the first publication of the work as a book in 1878. The library held both the periodical version and the Russian first edition, but Mr. Berger's knowledge of Russian was limited, to put it mildly, and he didn't think that it would be a good idea to go messing around with it in its original language. He decided that the library's first English language edition, published by Thomas Y. Crowell & Co. of New York in 1886, would probably be sufficient for his needs.

The weeks and months went by, but still he did not act. Not only was he afraid to put in place a plan that involved tinkering with one of the greatest works of literature in any language, but Mr. Gedeon was a perpetual presence in the library. He had not yet entrusted Mr. Berger with his own key, and he still kept a careful eye on his visitor. Meanwhile, Mr. Berger noticed that Anna was becoming increasingly agitated, and in the middle of their discussions of books and music, or their occasional games of whist or poker, she would grow suddenly distant and whisper the name of her children or her lover. She was also, he thought, taking an unhealthy interest in certain railway timetables.

Finally, fate presented him with the opportunity he had been seeking. Mr. Gedeon's brother in Bootle was taken seriously ill, and his departure from this earth was said to be imminent. Mr. Gedeon was forced to leave in a hurry if he was to see his brother again before he passed away and, with only the faintest of hesitations, he entrusted the care of the Caxton Private Lending Library & Book Depository to Mr. Berger. He left Mr. Berger with the keys, and the number of Mr. Gedeon's sister-in-law in Bootle in case of emergencies, then rushed off to catch the last evening train north.

Alone for the first time in the library, Mr. Berger opened the suitcase that he had packed upon receiving the summons from Mr. Berger. He removed from it a bottle of brandy, and his favorite fountain pen. He poured himself a large snifter of brandy—larger than was probably advisable, he would later accept—and retrieved the Crowell edition of Anna Karenina from its shelf. He laid it on Mr. Gedeon's desk and turned to the relevant section. He took a sip of brandy, then another, and another. He was, after all, about to alter one of the great works of literature, so a stiff drink seemed like a very good idea.

He looked at the glass. It was now almost empty. He refilled it, took another strengthening swig, and uncapped his pen. He offered a silent prayer of apology to the god of letters, and with three swift dashes of his pen removed a single paragraph.

It was done.

He took another drink. It had been easier than expected. He let the ink dry on the Crowell edition, and restored it to its shelf. He was, by now, more than a little tipsy. Another title caught his eye as he returned to the desk: *Tess of the d'Urbervilles* by Thomas Hardy, in the first edition by Osgood, McIlvaine and Co., London, 1891.

Mr. Berger had always hated the ending of *Tess of the d'Urbervilles*.

Oh well, he thought: in for a penny, in for a pound.

He took the book from the shelf, stuck it under his arm, and was soon happily at work on Chapters LVIII and LIX. He worked all through the night, and by the time he fell asleep the bottle of brandy was empty, and he was surrounded by books.

In truth, Mr. Berger had gotten a little carried away.

14

In the history of the Caxton Private Lending Library & Book Depository, the brief period that followed Mr. Berger's "improvements" to great novels and plays is known as the "Confusion" and has come to be regarded as a lesson in why such experiments should generally be avoided.

The first clue Mr. Gedeon had that something was amiss was when he passed the Liverpool Playhouse on his way to catch the train back to Glossom, his brother having miraculously recovered to such an extent that he was threatening to sue his physicians, and discovered that the theatre was playing *The Comedy of Macbeth*. He did a quick double-take, and immediately sought out the nearest bookshop. There he found a copy of *The Comedy of Macbeth*, along with a critical commentary labeling it "one of the most troubling of Shakespeare's later plays, due to its curious mixture of violence and inappropriate humor bordering on early bedroom farce."

"Good Lord," said Mr. Gedeon aloud. "What has he done? For that matter, what *else* has he done?"

Mr. Gedeon thought hard for a time, trying to recall the novels or plays about which Mr. Berger had expressed serious reservations. He seemed to recall Mr. Berger complaining that the ending of *A Tale of Two Cities* had always made him cry. An examination of a copy of the book in question revealed that it now ended with Sydney Carton being rescued from the guillotine by an airship piloted by the Scarlet Pimpernel, with a footnote advising that this had provided the inspiration for a later series of novels by Baroness Orczy.

"Oh, God," said Mr. Gedeon.

Then there was Hardy.

Tess of the d'Urbervilles now ended with Tess's escape from prison, engineered by Angel Clare and a team of demolitions experts, while *The Mayor of Casterbridge* had Michael Henchard living in a rose-covered cottage near his newly-married step-daughter and breeding goldfinches. At the conclusion of *Jude the Obscure*, Jude Fawley escaped the clutches of Arabella and survived his final desperate visit to Sue in the freezing weather, whereupon they both ran away and went to live happily ever after in Eastbourne.

"This is terrible," said Mr. Gedeon, although even he had to admit that he preferred Mr. Berger's endings to Thomas Hardy's.

Finally he came to *Anna Karenina*. It took him a little while to find the change, because this one was subtler than the others: a deletion instead of an actual piece of bad rewriting. It was still wrong, but Mr. Gedeon understood Mr. Berger's reason for making the change. Perhaps if Mr. Gedeon had experienced similar feelings about one of the characters in his care, he might have found the courage to intervene in a similar way. He had been a witness to the sufferings of so many of them, the consequences of decisions made by heartless authors, the miserable Hardy not least among them, but his first duty was, and always had been, to the books. This would have to be put right, however valid Mr. Berger might have believed his actions to be.

Mr. Gedeon returned the copy of *Anna Karenina* to its shelf, and made his way to the station.

15

Mr. Berger woke to the most terrible hangover. It took him a while even to recall where he was, never mind what he might have done. His mouth was dry, his head was thumping, and his neck and back were aching from having fallen asleep at Mr. Gedeon's desk. He made himself some tea and toast, most of which he managed to keep down, and stared in horror at the pile of first editions that he had violated the night before. He had a vague sense that they did not represent the entirety of his efforts, for he dimly recalled returning some to the shelves, singing merrily to himself as he went, although he was damned if he could bring to mind the titles of all the books involved. So ill and appalled was he that he could find no reason to stay awake. Instead he curled up on the couch in the hope that, when he opened his eyes again, the world of literature might somehow have self-corrected, and the intensity of his headache might have lessened. Only one alteration did he not immediately regret, and that was his work on *Anna Karenina*. The actions of his pen in that case had truly been a labour of love.

He rose to sluggish consciousness to find Mr. Gedeon standing over him, his face a mixture of anger, disappointment, and not a little pity.

"We need to have words, Mr. Berger," he said. "Under the circumstances, you might like to freshen up before we begin."

Mr. Berger took himself to the bathroom, and bathed his face and upper body with cold water. He brushed his teeth, combed his hair, and tried to make himself as presentable as possible. He felt a little like a condemned man hoping to make a good impression on the hangman. He returned to the living room and smelled strong coffee brewing. Tea, in this case, was unlikely to be sufficient for the task at hand.

He took a seat across from Mr. Gedeon, who was examining the altered first editions, his fury now entirely undiluted by any other emotions.

"This is vandalism!" he said. "Do you realize what you've done? Not only have you corrupted the world of literature, and altered the histories of the characters in our care, but you've damaged the library's collection. How could someone who considers himself a lover of books do such a thing?"

Mr. Berger couldn't meet the librarian's gaze.

"I did it for Anna," he said. "I just couldn't bear to see her suffer in that way."

"And the others?" said Mr. Gedeon. "What of Jude, and Tess, and Sydney Carton? Good grief, what of Macbeth?"

"I felt sorry for them, too," said Mr. Berger. "And if their creators knew that, at some future date, they might take on a physical form in this world, replete with the memories and experiences forced upon them, would they not have given some thought to their ultimate fate? To do otherwise would be tantamount to sadism!"

"But that isn't how literature works," said Mr. Gedeon. "It isn't even how the world works. The books are written. It's not for you or me to start altering them at this stage. These characters have power precisely *because* of what their creators have put them through. By changing the endings, you've put at risk their place in the literary pantheon and, by extension, their presence in the world. I wouldn't be surprised if we were to go back to the lodgings and find a dozen or more unoccupied rooms, with no trace that their occupants ever existed."

Mr. Berger hadn't thought of that. It made him feel worse than ever.

"I'm sorry," he said. "I'm so very, very sorry. Can anything be done?"

Mr. Gedeon left his desk and opened a large

cupboard in the corner of the room. From it he removed his box of restorer's equipment: his adhe-
sives and threads, his tapes and weights and rolls
of buckram cloth, his needles and brushes and
awls. He placed the box on his desk, added a number of small glass bottles of liquid, then rolled up
his sleeves, turned on the lamps, and summoned
Mr. Berger to his side.

"Muriatic acid, citric acid, oxalic acid, and Tar-
tureous acid," he said, tapping each bottle in turn.

He carefully mixed a solution of the latter three
acids in a bowl, and instructed Mr. Berger to apply
it to his inked changes to *Tess of the d'Urbervilles*.

"The solution will remove ink stains, but not
printer's ink," said Mr. Gedeon. "Be careful, and
take your time. Apply it, leave it for a few minutes,
then wipe it off and let it dry. Keep repeating until
the ink is gone. Now begin, for we have many
hours of work ahead of us."

They worked through the night, and into the
next morning. Exhaustion forced them to sleep for
a few hours, but they both returned to the task in
the early afternoon. By late in the evening, the
worst of the damage had been undone. Mr. Berger
even remembered the titles of the books that he
had returned to the shelves while drunk, although
one was forgotten. Mr. Berger had set to work on
making *Hamlet* a little shorter, but had got no further than Scenes IV and V, from which he had cut

a couple of Hamlet's soliloquies. The consequence was that Scene IV began with Hamlet noting that the hour of twelve had struck, and the appearance of his father's ghost. However by halfway through Scene V, and after a couple of fairly swift exchanges, it was already morning. When Mr. Berger's excisions were discovered many decades later by one of his successors, it was decided to allow them to stand, as she felt that *Hamlet* was quite long enough as it was.

Together they went to the lodgings and checked on the characters. All were present and correct, although Macbeth appeared in better spirits than before, and remained thus ever after.

Only one book remained unrestored: *Anna Karenina.*

"Must we?" said Mr. Berger. "If you say 'yes', then I will accept your decision, but it seems to me that she is different from the rest. None of the others are compelled to do what she does. None of them is so despairing as to seek oblivion over and over. What I did does not fundamentally alter the climax of the novel, but adds only a little ambiguity, and it may be that a little is all that she requires."

Mr. Gedeon considered the book. Yes, he was the librarian, and the custodian of the contents of the Caxton Private Lending Library & Book Depository, but he was also the guardian of its characters. He had a duty to them and to the books. Did one supersede the other? He thought of what Mr. Berger had said: if Tolstoy had known that, by his literary gifts, he would doom his heroine to be defined by her suicide, might he not have found a way to modify his prose even slightly, and thus give her some peace?

And was it not also true that Tolstoy's ending to the novel was flawed in any case? Rather than give us some extended reflection on Anna's death, he chose instead to concentrate on Levin's return to religion, Kozyshev's support for the Serbs, and Vronsky's commitment to the cause of the Slavs. He even gave the final word on Anna's death to Vronsky's rotten mother: "Her death was the death of a bad woman, a woman without religion." Surely Anna deserved a better memorial than that?

Mr. Berger had crossed out three simple lines from the end of Chapter XXXI:

The little muzhik ceased his mumblings, and fell to his knees by the broken body. He whispered a prayer for her soul, but if her fall had been unwitting then she was past all need of prayer, and she was with God now. If it were otherwise, then prayer could do her no good. But still he prayed.

He read the preceding paragraph:

And the candle by which she had read the book that was filled with fears, with deceptions, with an-

guish, and with evil, flared up with greater brightness
than she had ever known, revealing to her all that
before was in darkness, then flickered, grew faint, and
went out forever.

You know, thought Mr. Gedeon, Chapter XXXI
could end just as easily there, and there would be
peace for Anna.

He closed the book, allowing Mr. Berger's
change to stand.

"Let's leave it, shall we?" he said. "Why don't
you put it back on its shelf?"

Mr. Berger took the book reverently, and restored it gently, lovingly to its place in the stacks.
He thought about visiting Anna one last time, but
it did not seem appropriate to ask Mr. Gedeon's
permission. He had done all that he could for her,
and he hoped only that it was enough. He returned
to Mr. Gedeon's living room and placed the key to
the Caxton Library on the desk.

"Goodbye," he said. "And thank you."

Mr. Gedeon nodded but did not answer, and
Mr. Berger left the library and did not look back.

16

In the weeks that followed Mr. Berger thought
often of the Caxton Library, and of Mr. Gedeon,
and of Anna most of all, but he did not return to
the laneway, and he consciously avoided walking

near that part of the town. He read his books, and resumed his evening walks to the railway track. Each evening he waited for the last train to pass, and it always did so without incident. Anna, he believed, was troubled no more.

One evening, as summer drew to its close, there came a knocking on his door. He answered it to find Mr. Gedeon standing on his doorstep, two suitcases by his side, and a taxi waiting for him by the garden gate. Mr. Berger was surprised to see him, and invited him to step inside, but Mr. Gedeon declined.

"I'm leaving," he said. "I'm tired, and I no longer have the energy that I once had. It's time for me to retire, and entrust the care of the Caxton to another. I suspected as much on that first night, when you followed Anna to the library. The library always finds its new librarian, and leads him to its door. I thought that I might have been mistaken when you altered the books, and I resigned myself to waiting until another came, but slowly I came to understand that you were the one after all. Your only fault was to love a character too much, which caused you to do the wrong thing for the right reasons, and it may be that we both learned a lesson from that incident. I know that the Caxton and its characters will be safe in your care until the next librarian comes along. I've left a letter for you containing all that you need to know, and a number at which you can call me should you have any questions, but I think you'll be just fine."

He held out to Mr. Berger a great ring of keys. After only a moment's hesitation, Mr. Berger accepted them, and he saw that Mr. Gedeon could not stop himself from shedding a tear as he entrusted the library and its characters to its new custodian.

"I shall miss them terribly, you know," said Mr. Gedeon.

"You should feel free to visit us anytime," said Mr. Berger.

"Perhaps I will," said Mr. Gedeon, but he never did.

They shook hands for the final time, and Mr. Gedeon departed, and they did not meet or speak again.

17

The Caxton Private Lending Library & Book Depository is no longer in Glossom. At the beginning of this century the town was discovered by developers, and the land beside the library was earmarked for houses, and a modern shopping mall. Questions started to be asked about the peculiar old building at the end of the laneway, and so it was that one evening a vast fleet of anonymous trucks arrived driven by anonymous men, and in the space of a single night the entire contents of the Caxton Private Lending Library & Book Depository—books, characters and all—were spirited away and resettled in a new home in a little village not far from the sea, but far indeed from cities and, indeed, trains. The librarian, now very old and not a little stooped, liked to walk on the beach in the evenings, accompanied by a small terrier dog and, if the weather was good, by a beautiful, pale woman with long, dark hair.

One night, just as summer was fading into autumn, there was a knock on the door of the Caxton Private Lending Library & Book Depository, and the librarian opened it to find a young woman standing on the doorstep. She had in her hand a copy of *Vanity Fair*.

"Excuse me," she said, "I know this may sound a little odd, but I'm absolutely convinced that I just saw a man who looked like Robinson Crusoe collecting seashells on the beach, and I think he returned with them to this—" she looked at the small brass plate to her right—"*library*?"

Mr. Berger opened the door wide to admit her.

"Please come in," he said. "It may sound equally odd, but I think I've been expecting you . . ."